BUILD-A-BEAR WORKSHOP®

FURRY FRIENDS HALL OF FAME

The Official Collector's Guide

SCHOLASTIC INC.
New York Toronto London Auckland Sydney
Mexico City New Delhi Hong Kong Buenos Aires

Build-A-Bear Workshop®

Furry Friends Hall of Fame

The Official Collector's Guide

Maxine Clark

Founder and Chief Executive Bear

ISBN 0-439-88979-0

12 11 10 9 8 7 6 5 4 3 2 1 6 7 8 9 10 11/0

Printed in the U.S.A. 40

First Scholastic printing, September 2006

Hylas Publishing

Publisher: Sean Moore

Creative Director: Karen Prince

Project Manager: Sarah Reilly

Art Director: Gus Yoo

Designers: Marian Purcell and Sarah Reilly

Editorial Director: Gail Greiner

Editor: Suzanne Lander

Contributor: Staci Alfermann

Production: Sarah Reilly and Wayne Ellis

Build-A-Bear Workshop® Project Coordinator: Laura Kurzu

CONTENTS

WELCOME TO BUILD•A•BEAR WORKSHOP®

How The Store Came To Be

Build-A-Bear Workshop® was created on the simple premise that everyone, no matter age or gender, has a beary special place in their heart for their teddy bear. I know I do. My bear Teddy was my first best friend and helped shape me into the person I am today. I lost him when I was 10 years old and I've been looking for him ever since. In Build-A-Bear Workshop I know I've found that furbulous bear a million times over.

Teddy played a big part in inspiring Build-A-Bear Workshop, along with my young friends—Katie, who was 10-years-old at the time and her 7-year-old brother Jack, and of course their bears George and Teddy. In late 1996 Katie, Jack and I were on a hunt for Beanie Babies. When we couldn't find what we were looking for Katie said, "You know, we could make these." She meant that we should buy some plush fabric and beans and go home to do a craft project. But what I heard was a big idea with so much more potential. Suddenly, I'd found the inspiration for my new business. You know what they say, "Out of the mouths of babes." When I explained the idea to her she said "This is sooooo cool, we just have to do it." If she said "you" just have to do it, I don't know if I would have been as excited about it, but she was already engaged and imagining how much fun it was going to be!

When I was young, shopping was fun. It was an event. I would get dressed up and go to the department store with my Mother.

It wasn't about what we bought, it was about the experience. Those outings are some of my favorite childhood memories. I wanted to bring to life a place where families could come together to have fun and share experiences with their children.

I am beary proud of our teddy bear friends and how much joy they are spreading around the world. In this book, you'll get to know our furry friends, past and present. You'll hear a few of our stories, but the best stories will be the ones you experience for yourself with your cuddly stuffed friends.

Maxine Clark
Founder and Chief Executive Bear

THE BUILD·A·BEAR WORKSHOP® EXPERIENCE

Make Your Own Beary Special Friend

This book is stuffed with furry friends, stories of friendship, Bearisms™—little bits of teddy bear wisdom—and furbulous finds. So let's get started.

What makes a Build-A-Bear Workshop furry friend so special? You! You really bring the friend to life through the bear-making experience. Here's how it goes...

CHOOSE ME
Choose a friend to make from over 25 bears, dogs, bunnies and more.

HEAR ME
Let your bear do the talking by recording your own Build-A-Sound® message or adding a pre-recorded sound.

STUFF ME
Do a hug test to make sure it's stuffed just right.

STITCH ME
Fill it with good wishes and a heart—a Build-A-Bear Workshop® exclusive.

FLUFF ME
Fluff and brush the fur, too.

DRESS ME
Find the pawfect look from hundreds of outfits and accessories.

NAME ME
Give it a name and make a personalized birth certificate. Then enter it in the Find-A-Bear® ID system, so it can find its way home if lost.

TAKE ME HOME®
Recite The Bear Promise®, then walk out, hand-in-paw, with your new friend in an exclusive Cub Condo® carrying case!

THE BUILD•A•BEAR WORKSHOP® COLLECTION

The Bear Promise®

My bear is special
I brought it to life
I chose it,
I stuffed it
Now I am taking it home.
Best friends are forever
So I promise right now to make
my bear my #1 pal.

There are lots of furry friends to meet, so off we go...

BABY'S FIRST BLUE

intro date

This white teddy with blue stitching on its nose and paws is pawfect for baby's first bear. Fluffy as a cloud, this huggable bear is sure to be a friend furever.

vital stats

1 retirement date: June 98

2 height: 14 inches

3 fur color: white

4 fur type: fluffy

5 eye color: brown

FUN FACT

A furry friend is a beary special gift.
The best bear to give a child under three is a bare bear—undressed and totally huggable.

BABY'S FIRST PINK

intro date
OCT 97

This sweet friend gives a cuddly welcome into the world with its white fur and pink stitching on its nose and paws.

vital stats

1 retirement date: June 98

2 height: 14 inches

3 fur color: white

4 fur type: fluffy

5 eye color: brown

HUGS ARE THE LANGUAGE OF FRIENDSHIP

BLACK BEAR

intro date
OCT 97

This jet black bear is as dark as night, but loves to play with you all day.

VITAL STATS

1 retirement date: Jan 02

2 height: 15 inches

3 fur color: black

4 fur type: fluffy

5 eye color: brown

FUN FACT

Did you know we have a Cub Advisory Board—our original board of directors? It's made up of children who help us make beary important decisions on our furry friends, fashion and fun!

CHUBBY CUBBY®

intro date

Snuggling with this gentle giant is the beary best! Who could resist this shaggy, plump-bellied friend?

VITAL STATS

1 retirement date: Dec 00

2 height: 12 inches

3 fur color: chocolate

4 fur type: straight

5 eye color: brown

FUN FACT

Each furry friend is given a name by their new best pal. Rich D. from Glendale affectionately calls this friend Chubbis Cubbis.

CLASSIC BROWN TEDDY

intro date OCT 97

You'll have a history making friendship with this teddy that has velvety soft caramel colored fur! This timeless teddy is proud to be your friend.

VITAL STATS

1 retirement date: Feb 03

2 height: 11 inches

3 fur color: caramel

4 fur type: short

5 eye color: black

FUN FACT

Every furry friend receives a beary special heart ceremony where a red puffed heart is chosen, filled with wishes and then placed inside the animal, bringing the friendship to life.

CURLY BEAR

intro date OCT 97

This is one terrific teddy that loves to play! Adorable brown sugar fur, velvety button nose, and black paw pads make this teddy tops!

VITAL STATS

1 retirement date: Dec 02

2 height: 15 inches

3 fur color: brown sugar

4 fur type: curly

5 eye color: black

EVERYTHING IS PAWSIBLE WHEN YOU PUT YOUR MIND TO IT

CURLY BUNNY

intro date
OCT 97

This Bearrific® bunny hops right into your heart! With brown sugar fur, a velvety button nose, and beary cute ears, this is one funny bunny!

vital stats

1 retirement date: Dec 04

2 height: 15 inches

3 fur color: brown sugar

4 fur type: curly

5 eye color: black

THERE IS NO FRIEND LIKE AN OLD FRIEND

FLOPPY BEAR

intro date
OCT 97

One squeeze of this friend's squishy tummy and you'll see how cuddly a bear can be! With heather brown fur, this genuine teddy bear is a true treasure.

vital stats

1 retirement date: July 04

2 height: 18 inches

3 fur color: heather brown

4 fur type: short

5 eye color: black

FURRY OR FUZZY,
A HUG IS ALWAYS
BEARY NICE

FLOPPY COW

intro date
OCT 97

This cute cow wears a bell that lets you know it's on the scene. Smooches from this cow pal won't give you a milk mustache! It's udderly loveable!

VITAL STATS

1 retirement date: Mar 03

2 height: 18 inches

3 fur color: white & black

4 fur type: short

5 eye color: black

FUN FACT

On October 27, 1997, opening day of the beary first Build-A-Bear Workshop® store at Saint Louis Galleria, Rachel F. chose Milky the cow because she was so cute. Now she has over 20 Build-A-Bear Workshop friends, but Milky is still queen of her bedroom because she was the first!

FLOPPY DALMATIAN

This is one doggone cute canine. Our original spotted puppy is a beary playful pooch!

intro date OCT 97

VITAL STATS

1 retirement date: Mar 02

2 height: 18 inches

3 fur color: white & black

4 fur type: short

5 eye color: black

FUN FACT

One day, a sad-looking Floppy Dalmatian with a melted leg arrived at World Bearquarters. It was sent to us by a beary thankful Mom. That puppy had rested against a night light for hours. During the night, the mother checked on the child, noticed a strange odor and found the dog … melted, but not burning. Floppy Dalmatian's non-flammable material prevented a fire, saved the child and made one happy Mom!

FLOPPY FROG

intro date
OCT 97

This furbulous green frog has yellow webbed feet and wide eyes for scoping things out. This leapfrog-loving friend is right at home at your lily pad.

VITAL STATS

1 retirement date: May 01

2 height: 17 inches

3 fur color: green

4 fur type: smooth

5 eye color: black

WHAT MATTERS IS THE STUFF INSIDE

FLOPPY PIG

intro date
OCT 97

Think pink when you see this friend. With such an adorable face, this little piggy will go straight into your heart.

VITAL STATS

1 retirement date: Nov 99
2 height: 17 inches
3 fur color: pink
4 fur type: soft
5 eye color: black

IT'S NOT THE SIZE OF THE BEAR THAT COUNTS, IT'S THE SIZE OF ITS HEART

HUG ME BEAR

intro date

Always smiling and ready for a hug, this teddy with toasted vanilla colored fur and a pudgy tummy will melt your heart.

vital stats

1 retirement date: July 99

2 height: 20 inches

3 fur color: toasted vanilla

4 fur type: shaggy

5 eye color: black

FUN FACT

Did you know that if you're not getting three hugs a day, you're not giving three hugs a day? Think about it!

LIL' CUB® BUTTERSCOTCH

Small in size, but big in heart is this friend's theory. This teddy with butterscotch colored fur is a sweet treat.

intro date OCT 97

vital stats

1 retirement date: Aug 02

2 height: 14 inches

3 fur color: butterscotch

4 fur type: fuzzy

5 eye color: brown

FUN FACT

This teddy was not originally ordered, but came in by mistake as a lighter version of the taffy and chocolate colored fur. It was so cute, it stayed!

LiL' CUB® CHOCOLATE

intro date
OCT 97

There is more cuddle per square inch in this pint-sized pal—pawfect for hugging! You'll love this friend with chocolate colored fur. Yummy!

ViTAL STATS

1 retirement date: Aug 02

2 height: 14 inches

3 fur color: chocolate

4 fur type: fuzzy

5 eye color: brown

FUN FACT

The sweater this furry friend is wearing is mongrammed with "Teddy," in honor of Maxine Clark's first bear.

LIL' CUB® TAFFY

intro date
OCT
97

You'll find a friendship as yummy as candy with this taffy colored teddy. Satisfy your sweet tooth with this friend—cavity-free!

VITAL STATS

1 retirement date: Aug 02

2 height: 14 inches

3 fur color: taffy

4 fur type: fuzzy

5 eye color: brown

BEARS COUNT THEIR BLESSINGS ONE FRIEND AT A TIME

MiNK-LOOK BEAR

intro date
OCT 97

This traditional style teddy has a thoughtful expression and kind eyes to keep careful watch over you. Its mink-look fur is beary unique.

ViTAL STATS

1 retirement date: Dec 98
2 height: 18 inches
3 fur color: caramel
4 fur type: fluffy
5 eye color: brown

DON'T JUDGE A BEE BY iTS BUZZ

POLAR BEAR

intro date
OCT 97

This beary cool friend has long fluffy white fur to keep out the cold ... brrr! Its extra long arms give pawfect bear hugs to warm you.

VITAL STATS

1 retirement date: April 04

2 height: 21 inches

3 fur color: white

4 fur type: shaggy

5 eye color: brown

ONE GOOD BEAR DESERVES ANOTHER

SHAGGY BEAR

intro date
OCT 97

This shaggy bear lives by the motto—don't worry, be furry. It has a cool unkept look and casual attitude.

vital stats

1 retirement date: Nov 98

2 height: 18 inches

3 fur color: granola

4 fur type: shaggy

5 eye color: brown

LEAP INTO FURRY FUN EVERY DAY

Shaggy Dog

intro date
OCT 97

Ain't nothing but a … shaggy hound dog. It has cream fur, brown ears and tail, plus an extra-long nose for sniffing out clues and food that falls from the table.

vital stats

1 retirement date: Dec 01

2 height: 22 inches

3 fur color: cream & brown

4 fur type: shaggy

5 eye color: black

Go Fur It

Vintage Bear

intro date
OCT 97

This bear looks like it has already been loved! It has rumpled caramel fur with a brown embroidered nose.

Vital Stats

1 retirement date: Aug 00

2 height: 17 inches

3 fur color: caramel

4 fur type: curly

5 eye color: brown

Fun Fact

Perhaps the most famous Vintage Bear is Schaumburg. This adventuring friend is the subject of his own teddy bear newsletter written by Myke and Cathy Feinman from Illinois. Learn more about this terrific teddy at www.ifcomics.com

FLOPPY MONKEY

intro date
NOV 98

You'll have many adventures with this funky monkey. It's ready for the jungle or wherever you may roam with its thick brown fur, and long arms, legs and tail.

VITAL STATS

1 retirement date: July 03

2 height: 18 inches

3 fur color: chocolate

4 fur type: thick

5 eye color: black

REMEMBEAR THE SWEETS IN LIFE: FRIENDS, LOVE AND KINDNESS

BUNNY BIG EARS

intro date
FEB 99

With long furry ears and big paws for pouncing, this is a honey of a bunny! The fun begins when this friend filled with pawsonality shows up.

vital stats

1 retirement date: active

2 height: 18 inches

3 fur color: honey brown

4 fur type: fluffy

5 eye color: brown

BIG OR SMALL, ALWAYS CELE•BEAR•ATE YOUR ACCOMPLISHMENTS

PAWLETTE COUFUR®

Fashion Advisor To The Furry Famous

Pawlette Coufur is our Fashion Advisor to the Furry Famous. She was born on April 22 in a small carrot patch near Pawston, and soon found the world of furry fashion calling her name. She moved to Bearis and worked with all of the hot desingers, including Fuzzy, Grizz and Floppy. She soon became the final word on fashion for the furry.

BEAREMY®

intro date

Build-A-Bear Workshop® official mascot is ready to be your beary best friend! With "Bearemy" embroidered on its paw, this teddy shows you're a real bear lover!

VITAL STATS

1 retirement date: Active

2 height: 16 inches

3 fur color: heather brown

4 fur type: fuzzy

5 eye color: brown

THERE ARE NO LIMITS WHEN BEARS PUT THEIR MINDS TO IT

BEAREMY® MASCOT

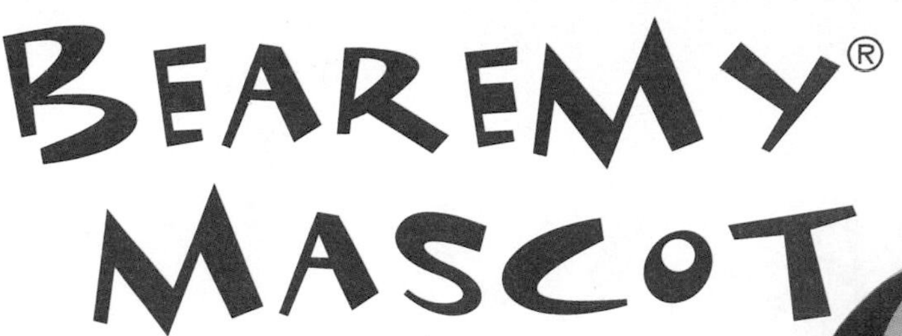

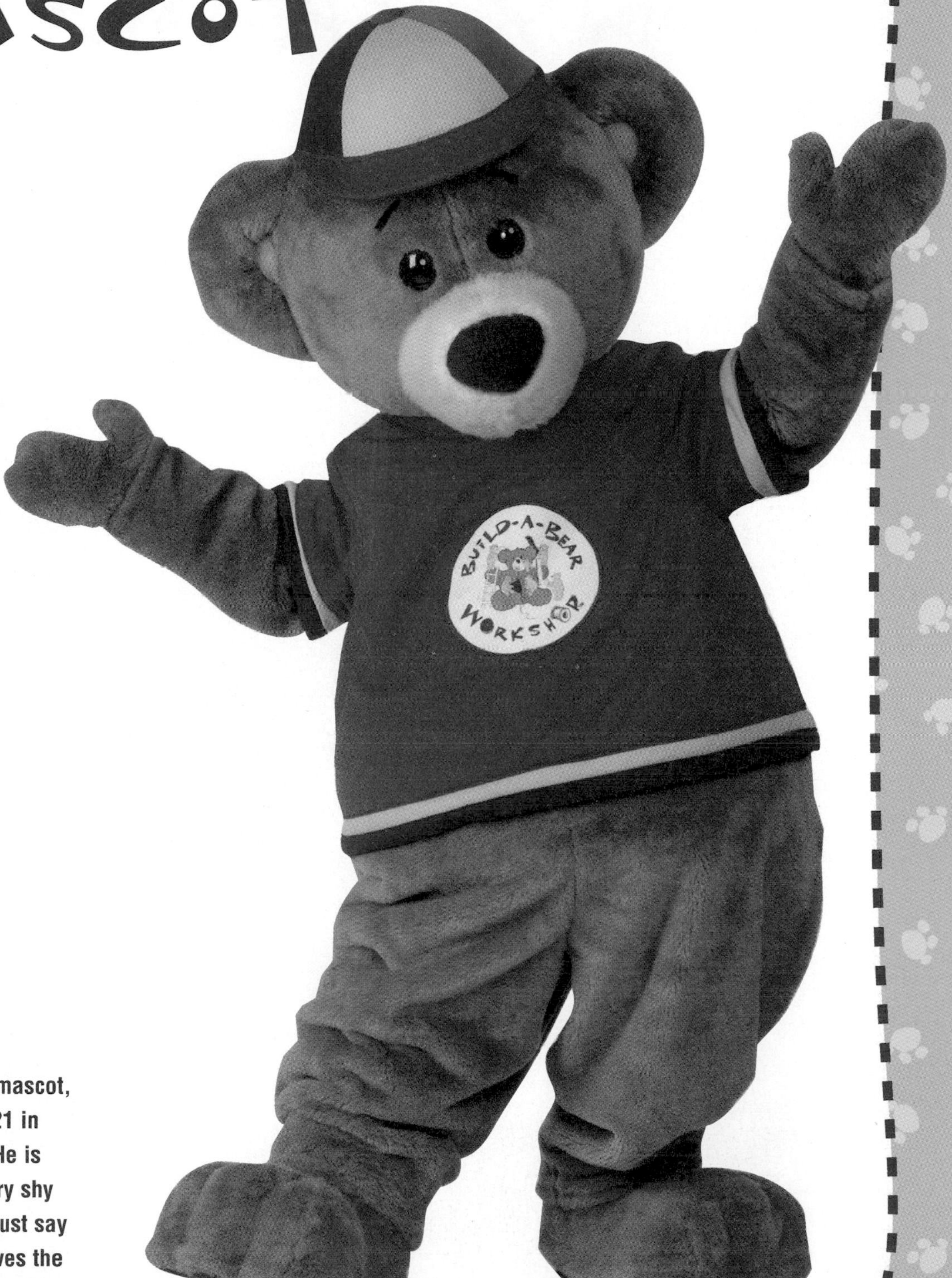

Bearemy, our huggable mascot, was born on August 21 in St. Louis, Missouri. He is 9 paws tall, but is beary shy about his weight. Let's just say he LOVES honey! He gives the best bear hugs you've ever had.

FLOPPY PONY CREAM

intro date
OCT 99

Our huggable stallion has just galloped in from the ranch. No horsing around, this cream-colored pal with ebony mane and tail is sweet.

VITAL STATS

1 retirement date: June 00

2 height: 17 inches

3 fur color: cream, white, black

4 fur type: soft

5 eye color: black

BE THE BEARER OF GOOD NEWS

FLOPPY PONY LIGHT BROWN

This chestnut friend with white face and ebony mane and tail is one pawsome pony. You'll have a galloping good time when this friend rides in.

intro date OCT 99

VITAL STATS

1 retirement date: July 05

2 height: 17 inches

3 fur color: tan, white, black

4 fur type: soft

5 eye color: brown

LIVE SIMPLY, LOVE WELL AND TAKE TIME TO TASTE THE HONEY ALONG THE WAY

KUDDLY KOALA®

intro date
MAR 00

G'day! Make a new friend with this sweet pal honoring all of our teddy bear mates from Down Under! You'll adore this gray-furred friend with a cute face.

vital stats

1 retirement date: Aug 02

2 height: 10 inches

3 fur color: light gray

4 fur type: fuzzy

5 eye color: blue-gray

FUN FACT

Starting in 2000, all furry friends and fashions had the Seal of Pawthenticity® — a heart and paw tag that shows they are a true Build-A-Bear Workshop® original!

GRIZZLY BEAR

intro date
MAR 00

Unique, mocha-tipped fur with a rich black undercoat make this a special furry friend indeed. Its round belly, arms and expression say, "Pick me up, please!"

vital stats

1 retirement date: Dec 01

2 height: 19 inches

3 fur color: mocha & black

4 fur type: shaggy

5 eye color: brown

FUN FACT

This year our patented pre-lace system was introduced—all animals were hand sewn closed until then!

FLOPPY TURTLE

intro date
APR 00

This terrific turtle has a removable shell backpack that holds cool stuff for all your adventures. Pack up and go play!

VITAL STATS

1 retirement date: Apr 04

2 height: 15 inches

3 fur color: green

4 fur type: smooth

5 eye color: black

FUN FACT

We know our furry friends attend lots of sleepovers, so we designed this one to carry its own stuff!

White Tiger

intro date
JULY
00

One look into its pawsitively piercing eyes and you're captured. With snow-white fur and charcoal stripes, this terrific tiger is surely a keeper.

Vital Stats

1 retirement date: active

2 height: 15 inches

3 fur color: white & black

4 fur type: fluffy

5 eye color: blue

Fun Fact

This was our first friend to be sold in select locations only. It's exclusively available in our Las Vegas area stores and at www.buildabear.com.

FLOPPY ELEPHANT

intro date
APR 01

This mighty mammal with soft gray fur will charge right into your heart. Big ears, trunk, and tusks are terrific and make this friend even more fun!

VITAL STATS

1. retirement date: May 03
2. height: 18 inches
3. fur color: gray
4. fur type: fuzzy
5. eye color: brown

IT DOESN'T HURT TO LET YOUR STUFFING SHOW

POLAR BEAR II

intro date
MAY 01

Warm your heart with
bear hugs in a BIG way
with this towering teddy.
You'll be loving large
with Polar Bear.

VITAL STATS

1 retirement date: Apr 04
2 height: 21 inches
3 fur color: white
4 fur type: shaggy
5 eye color: brown

FUN FACT

The first Polar Bear had stitching on its paws,
but this updated version has leather-like paw pads.

Grizzly Bear II

intro date

It's the softest grizzly you'll ever meet! Thick dark brown fur and warm brown eyes make this big cuddly bear a true friendship find.

vital stats

1 retirement date: Dec 02

2 height: 18 inches

3 fur color: dark brown

4 fur type: thick

5 eye color: brown

IT'S NEVER TOO LATE TO HAVE A HAPPY CHILDHOOD

BLACK BEAR II

intro date AUG 01

This friend is a real beauty with jet black fur and cream accents. It's a playful pal that looks ready to climb a tree and snag some honey.

vital stats

1 retirement date: Mar 04

2 height: 16 inches

3 fur color: black & cream

4 fur type: short

5 eye color: brown

JUST HUG

FLOPPY DALMATIAN II

intro date
NOV 01

You've spotted a life-long friend with this canine cutie that is lots of fun. It holds magnetic Bearemy's Kennel Pals® treats and toys in its mouth.

VITAL STATS

1. retirement date: Apr 04
2. height: 17 inches
3. fur color: white & black
4. fur type: fuzzy
5. eye color: black

FUN FACT

This canine companion was redesigned to be more interactive by adding a magnet to its mouth. Now all playful pups can hold treats and toys in their mouth!

FLUFFY PUPPY

intro date
NOV 01

You're in for a dog-gone good time with this pooch. This playful pup holds magnetic Bearemy's Kennel Pals® treats and toys in its mouth.

VITAL STATS

1 retirement date: Feb 05

2 height: 17 inches

3 fur color: cream & brown

4 fur type: shaggy

5 eye color: brown

DON'T FURGET TO LEND YOUR PAW TO A FRIEND IN NEED

CUDDLY TEDDY BLUE

intro date

With light blue nose and blue eyes, this is one beary cute teddy that babies will treasure. Super soft white fur makes for a lifetime of snuggling!

VITAL STATS

1 retirement date: active

2 height: 14 inches

3 fur color: white

4 fur type: fluffy

5 eye color: light blue

FUN FACT

"When I first started dating my husband, we went to the Build-A-Bear Workshop® in Memphis, Tennessee. I felt a little silly kissing the heart and making a wish seeing as I was an adult. My wish was that I would marry this wonderful man and a year later we were married. For our one-year anniversary, we stopped at the Knoxville, Tennessee store. We had just started trying to make a baby, so my wish was that I would get pregnant. And guess what ... I found out a month and a half later that I was four weeks pregnant! Who's to say wishing on my bears' hearts didn't have play in that somewhere?" —Sylvia B., Lexington, TN

CUDDLY TEDDY PINK

intro date
JAN
02

This special friend has soft white fur and a pink nose! It's the pawfect companion for a new baby.

VITAL STATS

1 retirement date: active

2 height: 14 inches

3 fur color: white

4 fur type: fluffy

5 eye color: brown

YOU AREN'T BORN A BEAR, YOU BECOME A BEAR

Curly Bear II

intro date
SEP 02

This classic-styled teddy with adorable curly fur is always a favorite friend.

vital stats

1 retirement date: active

2 height: 15 inches

3 fur color: brown sugar

4 fur type: curly

5 eye color: black

Fun Fact

Curly Bear II and Curly Bunny II arrived more relaxed—their fur that is. This style was their original design, but over the course of the years their fur just became more and more curly!

CURLY BUNNY II

intro date
SEP 02

This adorable friend with cute curly fur never has to worry about a bad hare day.

vital stats

1 retirement date: Aug 04

2 height: 15 inches

3 fur color: brown sugar

4 fur type: curly

5 eye color: brown

A SMILE IS THE BEST A BEAR CAN WEAR

PUDGIE PIG

intro date

This pink piggy is tickled to be your new best buddy. You'll be pig pals furever with this beary cute friend!

VITAL STATS

1 retirement date: Mar 05

2 height: 18 inches

3 fur color: pink

4 fur type: fuzzy

5 eye color: black

FUN FACT

This updated version of our original pig has bendable ears and super curly tail!

SHAGGY TEDDY

intro date
APR 03

This shaggy friend is ready to hug at a moment's notice. You'll be amazed by this friend's super-silky fur!

VITAL STATS

1 retirement date: active

2 height: 18 inches

3 fur color: heather brown

4 fur type: shaggy

5 eye color: brown

PAWS WERE MADE FUR HELPING

Marvelous Monkey

intro date

You'll go bananas over this funny friend! With sleek brown fur and long tail, this is one marvelous monkey with lots of pawsonality. No monkey business!

Vital Stats

1 retirement date: active

2 height: 18 inches

3 fur color: chocolate

4 fur type: sleek

5 eye color: black

Never Bear a Grudge

FLOPPY PONY II

intro date
JULY 03

Round up a great friendship with this playful pony with a chestnut coat. Ride off into the sunset for a lifetime of fun!

VITAL STATS

1 retirement date: active
2 height: 18 inches
3 fur color: chestnut
4 fur type: short
5 eye color: brown

FUN FACT

You make a personalized birth certificate for each new stuffed pal that commemorates the day you became best friends furever!

HAPPY CUB

This beary cute butterscotch-colored teddy is so happy to be your new best friend! This new pal will surely keep you smiling.

vital stats

1 retirement date: active

2 height: 15 inches

3 fur color: butterscotch

4 fur type: fuzzy

5 eye color: brown

HONEY IS MEANT TO BE GULPED NOT SIPPED

LIL' COCOA CUB

intro date
OCT 03

Start a big friendship with this little bear. Cuddly, cute and beary huggable, this cocoa-colored teddy is ready for fun.

vital stats

1 retirement date: active

2 height: 14 inches

3 fur color: cocoa

4 fur type: fuzzy

5 eye color: brown

FUN FACT

Thousands of friends have been reunited through our Find-A-Bear® ID system. We add a barcode to your friend, so if it gets lost and returned to Build-A-Bear Workshop®, we can scan the barcode and send it home to you.

UNICORN

intro date
NOV
03

This beautiful unicorn leads you to the magic of imagination and fantasy. Pretty pink-sparkle accents and pale blue eyes enhance the whimsical look of this furry friend.

VITAL STATS

1 retirement date: Mar 05

2 height: 18 inches

3 fur color: white & pink

4 fur type: sleek

5 eye color: black

FUN FACT

This was the first furry friend introduced that was a creature of fantasy, not a real animal.

LIL' CARAMEL CUB

intro date
NOV 03

Get cuddling with a caramel colored cutie! This huggable pal has been tasting the honey and has a tummy to show for it.

VITAL STATS

1 retirement date: active

2 height: 14 inches

3 fur color: caramel

4 fur type: fuzzy

5 eye color: brown

LIFE IS ALWAYS SWEETER WITH A LITTLE HONEY

Pink Poodle

intro date
DEC 03

A pretty pink pooch with curly fur makes the pawfect new friend! This playful pup holds magnetic Bearemy's Kennel Pals® treats and toys in its mouth.

Vital Stats

1 retirement date: active

2 height: 18 inches

3 fur color: pink

4 fur type: curly

5 eye color: brown

If it's meant to bee
it's up to me

TIE DYE TEDDY

intro date
JAN 04

This furry friend is bursting with color and energy! It's a groovy pal with red, yellow and orange tie-dyed shaggy fur.

VITAL STATS

1 retirement date: Jan 05

2 height: 16 inches

3 fur color: tie-dyed

4 fur type: shaggy

5 eye color: brown

FUN FACT

This was our first teddy with tie-dye-style fur, which became beary popular!

Floppy Gator

intro date
MAR 04

This beach-loving
Floppy Gator wants to
be your new best friend.
You'll have great gator
fun in the sun!

vital stats

1 retirement date: active

2 height: 18 inches

3 fur color: green

4 fur type: smooth

5 eye color: black

Fun Fact

This is a special friend that is only available in select beach locations.

MOCHA BUNNY

intro date

MAR 04

This happy hare will keep your life filled with warmth and overflowing with friendship. It's snuggly from the tip of its pink nose down to its fuzzy tail! Posing the ears is beary fun.

vital stats

1 retirement date: active

2 height: 16 inches

3 fur color: mocha

4 fur type: shaggy

5 eye color: brown

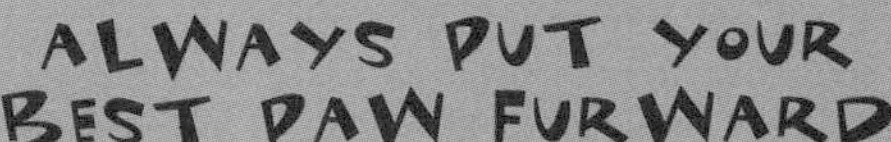

DiMPLES TEDDY

intro date
APR 04

This teddy spreads cheer wherever it goes with its smiling face and delightful dimples! It has beary cute and soft jet black fur with cream accents.

ViTAL STATS

1. retirement date: active
2. height: 16 inches
3. fur color: black
4. fur type: short
5. eye color: brown

HUGS ARE A BEAR ESSENTiAL

DIMPLES' ADVENTURE

"I wanted to let you both know that our love for Build-A-Bear Workshop® grew a little more today, even though I would not have believed that to be possible.

My middle daughter had lost one of her favorite Build-A-Bear Workshop animals at the mall last weekend. By the time she realized (a couple days later), I told her I was sorry but it was gone. (It took her a while to realize because the missing bear was "Dimples" and we also have the black bear with brown nose that looks the same but just slightly different that was out just before Dimples, so it is hard to keep track of them all—we have more than 30 Build-A-Bear Workshop friends!)

Anyway, she was very sad, but I reminded her that we were going there next week for her Daisy troop party and she would make a new friend. We were also going to look online or on E-bay for a "Dimples" to try to make up for it. I never dreamed that when UPS delivered a package that it would be her bear. She was so happy she literally cried, saying she thought it was thrown away or gone forever. She will be much more careful from now on, and will love Dimples a little more now, knowing the adventure he had while missing and how he came back to her.

I cannot thank you enough for this wonderful service you do, returning lost, loved friends. My daughter is a very happy girl because of you. We are die-hard fans, driving 40 minutes each way once a month to the Build-A-Bear Workshop (or more if there are good promotions!). Like I said, I didn't think I could think better of your company. You have a wonderful staff at our location (Eastview Mall, Victor, New York)—Renee and Shelby call my kids "cousins" when we come in because we are like family.

I didn't think I could love Build-A-Bear Workshop more, but seeing her toothless little smile made me so happy. So thank you again—this is a wonderful service you do and I can tell you that Build-A-Bear Workshop friends are the only stuffed animals we will ever buy again!"

Thank you sincerely,
Kristy M. (and Lexi M. too!)

MAPLE TEDDY

This big bear will be your best friend, protector and furvorite thing to hug! It's beary cute with thick maple-colored fur and leather-like paw pads.

VITAL STATS

1 retirement date: active

2 height: 20 inches

3 fur color: brown

4 fur type: thick

5 eye color: brown

A DAY WITHOUT HONEY IS UNBEARABLE

FRIENDLY FROG

intro date
JUNE 04

This great green friend will hop into your heart and fill your life with fun! Friendly and playful, it's ready for any adventure ... like catching flies. Ribbit!

VITAL STATS

1 retirement date: active

2 height: 17 inches

3 fur color: green

4 fur type: velvety

5 eye color: black

FUN FACT

This new version of the frog has much different eyes than the original, which had to be stuffed extra firm by hand!

Butterscotch Bear

intro date
JULY 04

This friend with butterscotch-colored fur is a beary yummy treat. You'll be hooked by its sweet bear hugs.

vital stats

1 retirement date: active

2 height: 14 inches

3 fur color: butterscotch

4 fur type: fluffy

5 eye color: brown

Fun Fact

Each new friend goes home in a Cub Condo® carrying case that is designed to be colored in by you to make it a beary unique new home.

intro date
JULY 04

Elmo came all the way from Sesame Street® to Build-A-Bear Workshop® to make new friends!

vital stats

1 retirement date: Dec 05

2 height: 18 inches

3 fur color: red

4 fur type: shaggy

5 eye color: black

SESAME STREET®

Sesame Workshop, the nonprofit educational organization behind Sesame Street, puts the proceeds it receives from sales of its products right back into Sesame Street and its other projects for children at home and around the world.

Learn more at www.sesameworkshop.org

SASSY KITTY

intro date
DEC 04

This fancy feline is filled with purr-sonality! Her sassy style shines through from her lashed eyes to her glitter tail. You'll adore her super-soft fur with purr-fect pink heart and accents.

VITAL STATS

1 retirement date: active

2 height: 18 inches

3 fur color: white

4 fur type: velvety

5 eye color: blue

FUN FACT

The story goes that Sassy Kitty was discovered by Pawlette Coufur®, Fashion Advisor to the Furry Famous, during Furry Fashion Week in Bearis. One look at this cool kitty, and she knew she had found the best shopping friend ever!

Velvet Teddy

intro date
APR 05

Once you touch this super-soft teddy you won't want to let go. Embroidered eyes and nose and velvety smooth fur make it the pawfect friend for kids of all ages.

Vital Stats

1 retirement date: active

2 height: 15 inches

3 fur color: cream

4 fur type: velvety

5 eye color: black

Fun Fact

By following the simple care instructions in the booklet attached to this friend, kids with asthma can now enjoy playing with stuffed toys without fear of increased incidence of asthma attacks.

CURLY TEDDY

intro date
MAY 05

This friend's soft curly fur, plump belly and velvety paw pads make it irresistible. Let the hugging begin!

VITAL STATS

1 retirement date: active

2 height: 15 inches

3 fur color: light brown

4 fur type: curly

5 eye color: brown

FUN FACT

Curly Teddy replaced Curly Bear as the friend featured in our dressed and ready to go Build-A-Gram® gifts at www.buildabear.com.

FURBULOUS FLAMINGO

intro date JUNE 05

This sun-lovin' friend has feather-look fur and soft velvety legs and beak. Being the only bird in the bunch doesn't keep this furry friend from strutting its stuff.

VITAL STATS

1 retirement date: Aug 05

2 height: 19 inches

3 fur color: pink

4 fur type: feather-look

5 eye color: green & black

FUN FACT

This Beary Limited™ edition Collectibear® friend was available summer 2005 only.

Build-A-Bear Workshop® Big Bears

It's Not The Size Of The Bear That Counts, It's The Size Of The Heart

Buddy Bear was the original towering teddy, introduced the first year we were open. A year later a brown version of this beary popular friend was created. Guests loved Buddy Bear and Big Brown Bear, which were about twice the size of most of our furry friends. That's a lot of cuddliness! These big bears had to have their own furbulous fashions because they were too large to fit in average bear-sized clothing. Small children could actually fit into their clothes. These friends retired in 1999, but their legend lives on today.

BUDDY BEAR

intro date
OCT 97

Buddy Bear was the biggest bear on the block when it came on the scene. It's the best kind of friend ... big and completely snuggly!

vital stats

1 retirement date: Feb 00

2 height: 28 inches

3 fur color: cream

4 fur type: fuzzy

5 eye color: black

A BEAR'S SMILE IS CONTAGIOUS

Big Brown Bear

intro date
JUNE
99

Big Brown Bear is one of the biggest bears in the bunch! You can take a nap on its belly, if you please. It's the bee's knees!

Vital Stats

1 retirement date: Dec 99

2 height: 28 inches

3 fur color: chocolate

4 fur type: fuzzy

5 eye color: black

THE WORLD IS A STAGE AND EVERY BEAR PLAYS ITS PART

BUILD-A-BEAR WORKSHOP® CENTENNIAL TEDDY BEARS

The 100th Annibearsary of the Teddy Bear

Build-A-Bear Workshop® proudly cele-bear-ated the Teddy Bear Centennial® with a Beary Limited™ edition Collectibear® series.

Did you know teddy bears received their name when the *Washington Post* printed a cartoon by Clifford K. Berryman depicting President Teddy Roosevelt refusing to shoot a bear which had been captured for him during a hunting excursion? A toy company, beary touched by the news, contacted the President and asked to use his name, Teddy, for their stuffed bear. The stuffed bear had been around for many years, but didn't have the official name Teddy Bear until 1902!

Centennial Teddy Bear 1

intro date
NOV 98

This Beary Limited™ edition Collectibear® friend makes a furever pal. First in the series, it has shaggy soft fur, leather-like paw pads and the jointed look of historic teddy bears.

Vital Stats

1 retirement date: July 00

2 height: 17 inches

3 fur color: caramel

4 fur type: shaggy

5 eye color: brown

Fun Fact

All of the Centennial Teddy Bears come with a Collector's Medallion.

CENTENNIAL TEDDY BEAR II

This Beary Limited™ edition Collectibear® friend makes a cuddly companion with swirly, soft fur, velvety paw pads and a jointed look reminiscent of teddy bears of the past.

intro date

VITAL STATS

1 retirement date: July 01

2 height: 17 inches

3 fur color: auburn

4 fur type: swirly

5 eye color: brown

Each friend in this series comes with a numbered Certificate of Authenticity.

CENTENNIAL TEDDY BEAR III

intro date
MAY 01

A rich golden brown, this Beary Limited™ edition Collectibear® friend has the jointed look of teddy bears of old, and a face that says your friendship will be eternal.

vital stats

1 retirement date: Sep 02

2 height: 19 inches

3 fur color: golden brown

4 fur type: fluffy

5 eye color: black

ASK NOT WHAT YOUR BEAR CAN DO FUR YOU, BUT WHAT YOU CAN DO FUR YOUR BEAR

CENTENNIAL TEDDY BEAR IV

Golden-tipped fur and jointed style make this regal Beary Limited™ edition Collectibear® friend a true piece of history.

intro date MAY 02

vital stats

1 retirement date: Dec 03

2 height: 18 inches

3 fur color: butterscotch

4 fur type: fuzzy

5 eye color: black

FUN FACT

This beary special bear in the series comes with a 12-page Historic Booklet outlining a few of a bear's furvorite things in history, a blue Collector's Medallion tied with pawtriotic ribbon and a Certificate of Authenticity.

Centennial Teddy Bear V

intro date
MAY 03

The final Beary Limited™ edition Collectibear® friend in the series saluting the Teddy Bear Centennial® has mogul fur, jointed style and chamois-like muzzle and paw pads.

Vital Stats

1 retirement date: June 04

2 height: 18 inches

3 fur color: butterscotch

4 fur type: curly

5 eye color: brown

Honey tastes sweeter when you share it with a friend

BUILD-A-BEAR WORKSHOP® CAUSE-RELATED BEARS

Beary Special Friends Help Important Causes

Teddy bears have big hearts! Build-A-Bear Workshop® is dedicated to making a difference in your community and the world by offering furry friends that support charitable efforts. When you make the friends on the following pages, a portion of the proceeds is donated to help their causes.

HOPEFUL WISHES TEDDY®

intro date AUG 01

$1 of the purchase of this beary special friend is donated to advance breast cancer research, education, screening and treatment.

VITAL STATS

1 retirement date: web only

2 height: 16 inches

3 fur color: pink tipped

4 fur type: fluffy

5 eye color: brown

FUN FACT

This friend came with a pink enamel ribbon breast cancer awareness pin.

TEDDY BEAR WISHES

One Girl's Wish Makes A Difference For Children With Cancer

Fourteen-year-old Nikki Giampolo loved life, loved children and loved teddy bears. She shared that love by giving bears and their hugs to all those around her. She lost her life to cancer in 2002, and her mom and friends shared her story of courage and hope with Build-A-Bear Workshop®. Nikki's story inspired us to create Nikki's Bear and to dedicate it to her wish of helping children with cancer. A portion of the proceeds from the sale of Nikki's Bear are distributed through the Build-A-Bear Workshop Foundation to fund children's health and wellness programs.

NIKKI'S NETWORK

Every year, 10,000 children in the United States are diagnosed with cancer. Nikki's Network is made up of kids all over the country who want to make a difference in their communities by helping other kids with cancer. To be part of Nikki's Network, visit the online fundraising tool kit on the Community Involvement section at www.buildabear.com to see how you can get involved and make a difference.

Nikki's Bear I

intro date
JAN 03

Nikki's Bear is a special friend that was created to honor a young girl who lost her life to cancer, but continues to inspire us every day.

vital stats

1 retirement date: July 04
2 height: 15 inches
3 fur color: purple tipped
4 fur type: fluffy
5 eye color: brown

Fun Fact

A portion of the proceeds from the sale of the Nikki's Bear series are donated to fund children's health and wellness initiatives through the Build-A-Bear Workshop Foundation.

NIKKI'S BEAR II

intro date
AUG 04

Nikki's Bear II is the second in a series and has helped raise funding and awareness for pediatric cancer, juvenile diabetes and autism research.

vital stats

1 retirement date: Sep 05

2 height: 16 inches

3 fur color: purple

4 fur type: fuzzy

5 eye color: black

FUN FACT

Nikki's Bear sends a message of hope and courage to children with cancer and is a celebration of life for those children and their families and friends who support them.

BUILD-A-BEAR WORKSHOP® BEARS THAT SUPPORT LITERACY

Teddy Bears And Books Have A Lot In Common

Just like teddy bears, books can carry kids of all ages off on adventures greater than they could ever imagine. That is why Build-A-Bear Workshop is proud to support literacy.

Read Teddy®

intro date JUNE 02

A portion of the proceeds from the sale of Read Teddy and Read Teddy II is donated to First Book to provide new books to children from low-income families and also to support other literacy organizations.

Vital Stats

1 retirement date: Feb 05

2 height: 16 inches

3 fur color: butterscotch

4 fur type: fuzzy

5 eye color: black

Fun Fact

When she was little, you could always find Build-A-Bear Workshop® Founder and Chief Executive Bear Maxine Clark tucked away in the library. It was her furvorite spot.

READ TEDDY® II

intro date
JAN 05

This furry friend is a beary good listener and makes a pawfect story-time companion.

VITAL STATS

1 retirement date: active

2 height: 16 inches

3 fur color: butterscotch

4 fur type: fuzzy

5 eye color: black

FUN FACT

Go to Bearemy's Book Club® at www.buildabear.com. You can read books featured on this beary fun site and see where they take you! Check out top recommended books, celebrity reviews and enter your own personal paw rating and review.

BUILD•A•BEAR WORKSHOP® BEAREMY'S KENNEL PALS®

Help Save Real Pets In Your Community

A portion of the proceeds from the sale of each full-sized Bearemy's Kennel Pals friend is donated by Build-A-Bear Workshop to support local animal shelters, stray pet rescue, and rehabilitation organizations. Money raised through the sales of these animals is directly granted to shelters and animal programs in the United States and Canada on a quarterly basis.
If your group would like to be considered for a cash grant from Build-a-Bear Workshop, go to www.buildabear.com to download a pet program grant application.

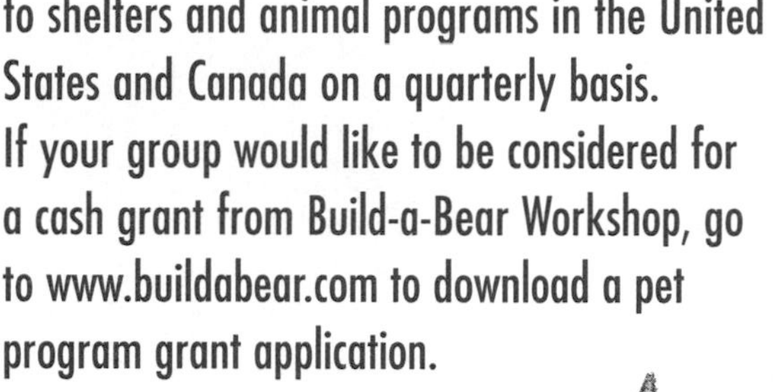

BLACK LABRADOR

intro date
SEP 01

This popular canine may have dark eyes and fur, but it has a beary bright pawsonality!

vital stats

1 retirement date: active

2 height: 16 inches

3 fur color: jet black

4 fur type: fuzzy

5 eye color: brown

FUN FACT

Bearemy's Kennel Pals® friends wear a collar and ID tag.

GOLDEN RETRIEVER

intro date
APR 02

Not even a kitty could resist this tongue-wagging pal with adorable golden fur.

vital stats

1. retirement date: Aug 04
2. height: 16 inches
3. fur color: golden blonde
4. fur type: shaggy
5. eye color: brown

Each playful pup in this collection holds magnetic Bearemy's Kennel Pals® treats, toys and Lil' Pals in its mouth.

WESTIE

intro date
OCT
02

Whether you're looking for a show dog or a playful pup, this wonderful snow-white friend is ready to go home with you.

VITAL STATS

1 retirement date: Dec 03

2 height: 19 inches

3 fur color: white

4 fur type: shaggy

5 eye color: brown

FUN FACT

This cool canine was inspired by a four-legged friend named Snickers that comes to work almost every day at World Bearquarters!

BEAGLE

intro date

MAY 03

One look into its sweet eyes and you'll see that a lifelong friendship with this delightful dog will hit the spot.

VITAL STATS

1 retirement date: active

2 height: 16 inches

3 fur color: tan, white, black

4 fur type: velvety

5 eye color: brown

GUARANTEED FLEA FREE

BORDER COLLIE

intro date
MAY 04

This is the pawfect companion—with soft, shaggy fur for petting, and big paws for pouncing and playing.

VITAL STATS

1 retirement date: active

2 height: 16 inches

3 fur color: black & white

4 fur type: shaggy

5 eye color: brown

FUN FACT

Play puppies make great gifts. You don't have to feed them because they are already stuffed!

YELLOW LABRADOR

intro date
OCT 04

This cute canine has perky ears and an expression that begs for you to come out and play.

VITAL STATS

1 retirement date: May 05

2 height: 16 inches

3 fur color: yellow

4 fur type: smooth

5 eye color: brown

YOU'RE ALL FLUFF
UNLESS YOU NURTURE
YOUR HEART STUFF

BOXER

intro date

From bringing you
your slippers to bringing
a smile to your face,
leave it to this
friendly fellow.

vital stats

1 retirement date: active

2 height: 16 inches

3 fur color: reddish brown

4 fur type: sleek

5 eye color: brown

FUN FACT

To cele-bear-ate an election year, Guests took to the polls and chose this top dog as the winner in our Guest's choice on-line election!

BUILD-A-BEAR WORKSHOP® WORLD WILDLIFE FUND SERIES

Making Friends That Make A Difference®

The call of the wild is for help for some animals. Make an animal in our World Wildlife Fund (WWF) series and Build-A-Bear Workshop donates $1 from the sale of each animal to WWF to protect animals from loss of habitat due to global warming and other factors, which include illegal hunting.

© WWF®

intro date
JULY
00

This plump and cuddly friend has black and white super-soft fur. Its beary cute face has distinctive black markings around the eyes.

VITAL STATS

1 retirement date: active

2 height: 15 inches

3 fur color: black & white

4 fur type: fuzzy

5 eye color: brown

FUN FACT

The Giant Panda, the symbol of WWF known worldwide, was the first animal in the series.

BENGAL TIGER

intro date AUG 01

With a sweet furry face and striped caramel and black fur, this terrific tiger is wildly friendly.

VITAL STATS

1 retirement date: Oct 02

2 height: 15 inches

3 fur color: caramel & black

4 fur type: fuzzy

5 eye color: brown

FUN FACT

Friends in the World Wildlife Fund series wear a Collector's Medallion.

LEOPARD

intro date
AUG 02

You've spotted one great pal in this loveable leopard. You'll be in for a life of wild times with this mountain dwelling friend.

VITAL STATS

1 retirement date: May 04

2 height: 16 inches

3 fur color: tan, brown, black

4 fur type: sleek

5 eye color: brown

FUN FACT

Each animal in this series comes with a Certificate of Authenticity by mail.

LION

intro date AUG 03

With all the markings of its friends in the wild right down to its shaggy tipped tail, this king of the jungle will be king of your heart.

VITAL STATS

1 retirement date: Jan 05

2 height: 16 inches

3 fur color: honey brown

4 fur type: sleek & shaggy

5 eye color: brown

FUN FACT

To reinforce the lesson of these beary important efforts, the stuffed animals in the World Wildlife Fund series closely resemble their real-life counterparts in the wild.

Polar Bear

With wonderful white fur and black accents, this freeze-friendly pal will warm any chilly day giving great bear hugs!

vital stats

1 retirement date: active

2 height: 16 inches

3 fur color: white

4 fur type: fluffy

5 eye color: black

Fun Fact

For more information on other ways you can help World Wildlife Fund, visit www.worldwildlife.org.

BEARY LIMITED™ EDITION COLLECTIBEAR® AND COLLECTIBUNNY® FRIENDS

Each holiday season we introduce a friend that is around for a beary short time to cele-bear-ate!

NEW YEARS

Ring In The New Year With Friends

MiLLENNiUM CUB

intro date OCT 99

A unique friend indeed, this teddy has snow-white fur with iridescent sparkles, crystal blue eyes and a shiny silver nose.

ViTAL STATS

1 retirement date: Dec 99

2 height: 11 inches

3 fur color: white iridescent

4 fur type: fluffy

5 eye color: blue

FUN FACT

This Beary Limited™ edition Collectibear® friend commemorating the new millennium has "2000" embroidered on its paw and comes with a Collector's Medallion.

NEW YEAR BEAR

intro date
OCT 00

With cool blue fur, gold accents and Collector's Medallion, this Beary Limited™ edition Collectibear® friend is sure to bring blue skies all year.

VITAL STATS

1 retirement date: June 01
2 height: 10 inches
3 fur color: blue
4 fur type: furry
5 eye color: brown

BE KIND,
BE TRUE,
BEE HONEY

VALENTINE'S DAY

Love Is The Stuff Inside®

LIL' LUV CUB

intro date
DEC 98

This Beary Limited™ edition Collectibear® friend is filled with love, from its snow-white paws to the tip of its heart-shaped nose.

VITAL STATS

1 retirement date: Mar 99
2 height: 10 inches
3 fur color: snow white
4 fur type: fluffy
5 eye color: brown

OPEN YOUR PAWS TO LOVE

A Beary Limited™ edition Collectibear® friend, this snow white teddy shows its heart inside and out, even on its paws.

vital stats

1 retirement date: Feb 00

2 height: 10 inches

3 fur color: snow white

4 fur type: fluffy & textured

5 eye color: brown

LOVE IS PAWSITIVELY PRECIOUS

LIL' LOVE CUB

intro date
NOV 00

This friend has a beary special space in its heart to carry your Valentine's gift. With red nose and paw pad accents, this Beary Limited™ edition Collectibear® friend is a heart melter.

vital stats

1 retirement date: Feb 01

2 height: 13 inches

3 fur color: white

4 fur type: fuzzy

5 eye color: brown

FUN FACT

The Be Mine Heart is a removable backpack, too.

HEART CUB

intro date
DEC 01

This Beary Limited™ edition Collectibear® friend has pure white fur with red nose, red heart and heart-shaped paw pads.

VITAL STATS

1 retirement date: Feb 02

2 height: 10 inches

3 fur color: white

4 fur type: fluffy

5 eye color: black

WHEN IT'S DARK, LET THE LOVE IN YOUR HEART LIGHT THE WAY

KISSES FUR YOU® TEDDY

This loveable teddy blows kisses with its magnetic mouth and paws! It's a Beary Limited™ edition Collectibear® friend with super soft white fur with red heart accents.

intro date DEC 02

VITAL STATS

1 retirement date: Feb 03

2 height: 15 inches

3 fur color: white

4 fur type: fluffy

5 eye color: black

THE FUR MAY FADE BUT THE LOVE LASTS FUREVER

HEARTS-A-PLENTY TEDDY

intro date
DEC 03

This teddy with snow-white fur and red hearts sends wishes of hugs and kisses! This Beary Limited™ edition Collectibear® friend has magnetic mouth and paws to blow kisses.

VITAL STATS

1 retirement date: Feb 04
2 height: 15 inches
3 fur color: white
4 fur type: fuzzy
5 eye color: brown

BEARS LIVE BY THE RULES OF THE HEART

VALENTINE'S HUGS TEDDY

intro date
DEC 04

This snuggly teddy warms your heart! A Beary Limited™ edition Collectibear® friend, it has a magnetic mouth and paws to give kisses, red suede-like accents and "HUGS" embroidered on its paw.

VITAL STATS

1 retirement date: Feb 05

2 height: 14 inches

3 fur color: white

4 fur type: silky

5 eye color: black

HUG A BEAR AND BRING YOUR HEART TO LIFE

ST. PATRICK'S DAY

Luck O' The Bearish®

LIL' O'CUB®

intro date
FEB
00

This special bear has bright white fur with a shamrock on the tummy, emerald green eyes and shiny gold nose. Erin go bear!

vital stats

1 retirement date: Mar 00

2 height: 13 inches

3 fur color: white

4 fur type: fuzzy

5 eye color: brown

FUN FACT

"2000" is embroidered on the paw of this Beary Limited™ edition Collectibear® friend.

McBearish

intro date

With kelly green fur and embroidered paw shamrock, this Beary Limited™ edition Collectibear® friend will lead you to the pot of honey at the end of the rainbow.

Vital Stats

1 retirement date: Mar 01

2 height: 13 inches

3 fur color: kelly green

4 fur type: fuzzy

5 eye color: black

A Bear Hug is Worth a Thousand Words

LIL' LUCK CUB®

intro date
JAN 02

This fluffy green Beary Limited™ edition Collectibear® friend brings luck your way. With a shamrock printed on its paw—it must be the luckiest bear of all!

VITAL STATS

1 retirement date: Mar 02

2 height: 10 inches

3 fur color: green

4 fur type: shaggy

5 eye color: brown

BEARS ARE MEASURED BY THE SIZE OF THEIR HEARTS

LUCKY TEDDY

intro date

Direct from the end of the rainbow, this Beary Limited™ edition Collectibear® friend is ready to grant your wishes! Snow-white fur with green shamrocks make this pal pawfect for St. Patrick's Day.

VITAL STATS

1 retirement date: Mar 03

2 height: 15 inches

3 fur color: white

4 fur type: fuzzy

5 eye color: green

A BEAR WILL WALK A MILE FUR A FRIEND

TEDDY O'SHAMROCK

This teddy sham-rocks! It has snow-white fur, a shamrock on its belly, and green paw pads, nose and eyes. You're in for a lucky ride with this Beary Limited™ edition Collectibear® friend.

intro date FEB 04

VITAL STATS

1. retirement date: Mar 04
2. height: 15 inches
3. fur color: white
4. fur type: fuzzy
5. eye color: green

FRIENDSHIP IS A GIFT FUR ALL SEASONS

Lucky O'Teddy

intro date

FEB 05

Luck is just around the corner with this Beary Limited™ edition Collectibear® friend. This bright green teddy with a shamrock on its paw is filled with Irish charm!

vital stats

1 retirement date: Mar 05

2 height: 15 inches

3 fur color: green

4 fur type: fluffy

5 eye color: green

Bears Who are Loved are Bears in Luck

SPRING

Hop Into Furry Fun

LiL' BUNNY

intro date
OCT 97

This un-bear-lievably soft bouncing bunny has floppy ears, a sweet face and paws that were made for hopping! This Beary Limited™ edition Collectibunny® friend hops right into your heart.

VITAL STATS

1 retirement date: Apr 98

2 height: 11 inches

3 fur color: honey brown

4 fur type: soft

5 eye color: black

FUN FACT

This adorable animal was the beary first Collectibunny® friend!

FLUFFY BUNNY

intro date
NOV 98

This Beary Limited™ edition Collectibunny® friend is marshmallowy soft and fluffy. It is white as a late spring snow shower, with a cottony tail and pink paw pads.

VITAL STATS

1 retirement date: June 99
2 height: 10 inches
3 fur color: white
4 fur type: fluffy
5 eye color: black

SOME BUNNY LOVES YOU

CHOCOLATE BUNNY

intro date
JAN 00

This Beary Limited™ edition Collectibunny® friend looks good enough to eat! It has chocolaty fur and peach accents. This huggable hare makes the pawfect springtime pal.

VITAL STATS

1 retirement date: July 00

2 height: 10 inches

3 fur color: chocolate

4 fur type: fluffy

5 eye color: brown

FUN FACT

You can pose this friend's beary cute ears.

LIL' BUNNY II

intro date
DEC 00

This freckle-faced furry friend will bounce right into your heart. This Beary Limited™ edition Collectibunny® friend is a pawsome pal for spring.

VITAL STATS

1 retirement date: Dec 01

2 height: 15 inches

3 fur color: cream

4 fur type: fuzzy

5 eye color: forest green

FUN FACT

Although called "lil'," this Collectibunny® friend was full size at 15 inches.

JOYFUL BUNNY®

intro date

Spring into fun with a bunny friend. Chocolate marbled fur makes this Beary Limited™ edition Collectibunny® friend unique.

vital stats

1 retirement date: Apr 02

2 height: 15 inches

3 fur color: chocolate marble

4 fur type: fuzzy

5 eye color: black

FUN FACT

This bunny looks like it fell into a cup of cocoa to get its beary cute coloring!

LIL' FLOPPY BUNNY

intro date
MAR
03

This un-bear-lievably soft bunny has chamois ears, face and paws. This Beary Limited™ edition Collectibunny® friend is the pawfect companion for spring fun!

vital stats

1 retirement date: Apr 03

2 height: 17 inches

3 fur color: brown

4 fur type: furry

5 eye color: black

REACH FUR THE STARS

SPRING CHICK

intro date
FEB 04

Cele-bear-ate spring with a super fuzzy chick as your new best friend. Hatch a plan for fun with this Beary Limited™ edition Collectibear® friend.

VITAL STATS

1 retirement date: June 04

2 height: 17 inches

3 fur color: yellow

4 fur type: fluffy

5 eye color: black

FUN FACT

This was the beary first springtime friend that wasn't a bunny!

VANILLA FUDGE BUNNY

Fluffy fur, big floppy ears and squishy belly make this Beary Limited™ edition Collectibunny® friend a treat.

intro date FEB 05

VITAL STATS

1 retirement date: active

2 height: 16 inches

3 fur color: chocolate marble

4 fur type: soft

5 eye color: brown

PAWSITIVE STUFF HAPPENS ONE PAW AT A TIME

LOVEABLE LAMB

intro date
MAR 05

VITAL STATS

1 retirement date: May 05

2 height: 16 inches

3 fur color: white

4 fur type: shaggy

5 eye color: black

This Beary Limited™ edition Collectibear® friend is the pawfect friend with soft, huggable fur, velvety paws and a cute smiling face.

FALL

Tricks, Treats and Friends to Meet

LUCKY KITTY®

intro date
AUG 99

This slick black kitty with a bright orange nose is a treat, no trick! When this Beary Limited™ edition Collectibear® friend crosses your path, you're in for some fun.

vital stats

1 retirement date: Nov 99

2 height: 16 inches

3 fur color: black

4 fur type: sleek

5 eye color: green

REMEMBEAR: INSIDE IS THE BEST OF ME–REAL HEART DETERMINES MY DESTINY

HALLOWEEN CUB

intro date
AUG 00

You'll scream with delight this Beary Limited™ edition Collectibear® friend is so frightfully cute! It has glow-in-the-dark eyes, black fur with silver shimmer, a pumpkin-patch paw and an orange nose.

vital stats

1 retirement date: Nov 00

2 height: 11 inches

3 fur color: black & silver

4 fur type: fuzzy

5 eye color: glow in the dark

FUN FACT

This unique friend was the first with shimmer in its fur and glow-in-the-dark eyes.

HALLOWEEN CUB II

intro date
AUG 01

Glow-in-the-dark eyes and black fur with orange glitter give this bear flair, not scare. This Beary Limited™ edition Collectibear® friend is a boo-rrific Halloween pal.

VITAL STATS

1 retirement date: Mar 02

2 height: 15 inches

3 fur color: black & orange

4 fur type: furry

5 eye color: glow in the dark

FUN FACT

Halloween Cub's glow-in-the-dark eyes and shimmer fur were so popular, we updated this year's friend with glitter fur.

BLACK CAT

intro date
AUG 02

This Beary Limited™ edition Collectibear® friend makes the purr-fect Halloween friend. It has the word "Boo" embroidered on its paw and orange accents.

VITAL STATS

1 retirement date: Oct 03

2 height: 16 inches

3 fur color: black

4 fur type: shaggy

5 eye color: glow in the dark

I NEVER MET A TEDDY I DIDN'T LIKE

HAPPY HARVEST TEDDY

intro date
SEP 03

This Beary Limited™ edition Collectibear® friend cele-bear-ates fall fun. This huggable friend is pawfect for snuggling when the weather turns chilly.

VITAL STATS

1 retirement date: Nov 03

2 height: 15 inches

3 fur color: orange

4 fur type: fluffy

5 eye color: brown

FUN FACT

This was our beary first orange Collectibear® friend.

FESTIVE FALL TEDDY

intro date
SEP 04

This is one outrageous orange fall friend. You can't help but smile when this ultra-soft Beary Limited™ edition Collectibear® friend is there to hug.

VITAL STATS

1 retirement date: Nov 04

2 height: 15 inches

3 fur color: orange

4 fur type: silky

5 eye color: black

REMEMBEAR YOUR BEARY FIRST TEDDY

HOLIDAY

Where Best Gifts Are Made®

FLOPPY MOOSE

Teddy bears love to befriend all animals. Our beary first moose came on the scene to cele-bear-ate the holidays. It is a Beary Limited™ edition Collectibear® friend.

intro date
OCT 98

vital stats

1 retirement date: Dec 98

2 height: 16 inches

3 fur color: chocolate

4 fur type: furry

5 eye color: black

GIVE GOOD STUFF

PERKY PENGUIN®

intro date

Sporting a red scarf, this Beary Limited™ edition Collectibear® friend is ready for chilly weather. With chubby cheeks and a cheery smile, our marshmallow-soft friend waddles into your heart.

VITAL STATS

1 retirement date: Jan 00

2 height: 12 inches

3 fur color: black & white

4 fur type: short

5 eye color: brown

FRIENDS MAKE THE HOLIDAYS BEARY BRIGHT

KUDDLY KITTY

intro date
NOV 00

Beary Limited™ edition Collectibear® Kitty and Mouse are purr-fect pals. During the cold winter months, Mouse snuggles warmly in Kitty's velvety fur.

VITAL STATS

1 retirement date: July 02

2 height: 16 inches

3 fur color: white & red

4 fur type: velvety

5 eye color: blue

FUN FACT

Kitty wears a heart-shaped Collector's Medallion that can be personalized with letter stickers.

CHOCOLATE MOOSE

intro date
OCT 01

This mighty moose with dark eyes is a real holiday catch! It has chocolate brown fur and textured antlers and paws that are un-bear-lievably soft.

VITAL STATS

1 retirement date: Jan 02

2 height: 15 inches

3 fur color: chocolate

4 fur type: fuzzy

5 eye color: black

FUN FACT

This mighty moose is a Beary Limited™ edition Collectibear® friend.

PLAYFUL PENGUIN

intro date
NOV 02

Chill out with this
Beary Limited™ edition
Collectibear® friend.
This freeze-friendly pal
is playfully pawfect!

VITAL STATS

1 retirement date: Jan 03

2 height: 18 inches

3 fur color: black & white

4 fur type: smooth

5 eye color: brown

FURRY FRIENDS WARM CHILLY DAYS

HOLIDAY REINDEER

intro date
NOV 03

This prancing reindeer flew in direct from the North Pole. Super soft antlers and spotted coat make this friend a holiday treat.

vital stats

1 retirement date: Jan 04

2 height: 18 inches

3 fur color: brown & white

4 fur type: soft

5 eye color: brown

IT'S BETTER TO GIFT THAN RECEIVE

RUDOLPH THE RED-NOSED REINDEER®

intro date
NOV 04

This holiday classic cele-bear-ates the 40th anniversary of the treasured movie—*Rudolph the Red-Nosed Reindeer®*.

vital stats

1 retirement date: Dec 04

2 height: 18 inches

3 fur color: reddish brown

4 fur type: velvety

5 eye color: black

FUN FACT

This Beary Limited™ edition Collectibear® friend is complete with light-up nose, of course.

Build-A-Bear Workshop® International Collectiwear™ Series

A Bear Hug Is Understood In Any Language

Build-A-Bear Workshop is making smiles around the globe with stores open in Australia, Denmark, France, Japan, South Korea and the United Kingdom, with Taiwan, Sweden, Norway and The Netherlands stores to come soon! To cele-bear-ate our global expansion, Guests can create their own united nations of bears by dressing friends in our international Collectiwear™ series — exclusively available in the biggest Build-A-Bear Workshop store in the world — New York City on 5th Ave at 46th! Each authentic outfit comes with a collectible numbered mini-passport telling why it's beary important to that culture.

These Beary Limited™ Edition outfits are featured on the following pages.

1

2

3

4

1 CAFTAN

When African girls go to get dressed,
They pick out the caftan that they like best.
Choosing a colorful traditional-style gown,
Topping it off with a headdress as lovely as a crown.

2 EGYPTIAN QUEEN

In Egypt the queen ruled the land,
She reigned over the people of the great sand.
The pyramids bowed to her beauty and grace,
Her power gave her in history a place.

3 ADVENTURER

From a safari outing to white-water rafting,
No telling what adventure he's crafting.
His khaki shorts and vest are his signature style,
Keeping him comfy as he travels a long while.

4 HULA DANCER

A tropical paradise is the stage,
For the hula dance, at any age.
A shake of the hips and wave of the hands,
It's beary popular on the Hawaiian Islands.

5 CHEONGSAM

Meaning "long dress" in Chinese,
Its grace and beauty surely please.
Started as a traditional style, it's told,
Now worn worldwide by young and old.

6 HANBOK

Hanbok is traditional wear in a Korean house.
Chima is the skirt and Chogori is the blouse.
Its bright colors make it a favorite, you'll see,
It even comes with a headpiece and bag accessory.

7 KiMONO GiRL

When you see a kimono you can surely tell
the age of the girl and the season as well.
The garment is traditional Asian style
Worn since the 1600s—that's a beary long while!

8 KiMONO BOY

When samurais fought, the land was lush.
Hakama "pants" protected legs from brush.
They were worn with the kimono, it's true,
Which was usually a dark color, like blue.

9

10

11

12

9 KURTA & PYJAMA OUTFIT

A kurta is a flowing top that's long,
Paired with pyjamas—no, that's not wrong.
These pyjamas are a special kind of pants
You can wear them all day long, even when you dance!

10 QUEEN

Dressed in royal purple from head to toe,
Being queen is the way to go!
Topped with a crown of pearls and gold,
She is loved by the young and the old.

11 KING

Being king is the way to go,
Dressed in velvet from head to toe!
Topped off with a regal crown,
Royalty are the best dressed in town!

12 PALACE GUARD

The palace guard watches over the king and queen,
Making sure no danger goes unseen.
They protect the rest of the community too.
That's a beary big job to do!

13 Royal Guard

The tower is a beary special place
Where you will see the royal guard pace.
They watch over the royal jewels too.
That's a beary important job to do!

15 Poet

A poet is a writer true,
It's in their blood, it's what they do.
They rhyme, they muse, they compose,
They create Bearrific® prose.

14 Royal Musician

The royal musician plays all day,
Beating his drum along the way.
He drums at the palace for the king and queen,
And everywhere in town he can be seen.

16 Euro Flower Girl

In Northern Europe flowers bloom free,
Their beauty abounds for all to see.
Traditional outfits blossom in floral wear
Flowers from head to toe on a maiden fair.

17

18

19

20

17 ALPINE BOY

Traditional folk dancers perfom across the land,
Usually accompanied by a Bavarian band.
Their costume, called tracht, is from the 19th century
found in Austria, Switzerland, and Germany.

19 FRENCH CANCAN

The music halls of Paris were alive,
With cancan dancers, they did thrive.
Outrageous costumes filled the stage.
Glitz, glam and glitter were the rage.

18 CHEF LE BEAR

A sprinkle of "wow," a dash of yummy,
The gourmet chef delights the tummy.
Stirring, tasting, baking and more,
This is one chef everyone will adore!

20 GONDOLIER

In Venice the Gondoliers row to and fro,
Serenading their passengers as they go.
Providing a service of transportation,
They are famous across every nation.

21 HIGHLANDER

In Scotland, highland men play proudly,
Blowing their bagpipes beary loudly.
They wear skirts, called kilts it's true.
It's a beary traditional thing to do.

22 EASTERN EUROPEAN GIRL

Beautifully crafted dresses trimmed in gold,
Reminding us of times of old.
Traditionally colored—blue and red,
With a veiled cap for her head.

23 EASTERN EUROPEAN BOY

Traditionally crafted outfit, so it's told,
Reminding us of times of old.
With velvet pants and rope tie too,
It is topped off with a regal cape of blue.

24 VIKING

Early in history, raiders swept the land.
They were warrior men with a heavy hand,
Coming from Scandinavia and traveling by sea,
Oh they were quite a sight to see!

25 IRISH DANCER

Today's Irish dancer's dress is traditional wear
Based on 200 year ago peasant lasses' fare.
Each school of dance has its own costume, true,
With Celtic designs and its own coloring too.

27 BULLFIGHTER

The bullfighter is brave and strong,
Charging at the bulls all day long.
Waving his red cape as the crowd cheers loudly,
He is a hero and shows it off proudly.

26 FLAMENCO DANCER

Flamenco dancers are full of pep,
Feeling the music in every step.
Rapidly clapping and chanting loudly
They rule the dance floor beary proudly.

28 GAUCHO OUTFIT

A gaucho is a cowboy true,
A skillful horseman and beary strong too.
In South America they ride the range all day,
The pampas are their lands to protect and play.

29 SAMBA DANCER

Feel the hot samba beat,
Dancers can't help but move their feet.
Dressed brightly in stripes and polka dots on red,
Topped off with a fruit wrap on the head.

30 LATIN AMERICAN GIRL

Girls' outfits in South America and Mexico
Display a bit of "cultura" wherever they go.
Folk art embroidered flowers and ruffles they wear,
Giving their blouse, skirt and shawl a festive flair.

31 MARIACHI

Mariachi is music that comes from the soul
With beautiful costumes for all to behold.
Imagine those singers and instruments too,
As they come to your window to serenade you!

32 GODDESS

In mythology the goddesses ruled on high,
Watching over the world all day and into the nigh'.
Beaming with beauty and filled with grace,
They were worshipped by the human race.

33

34

35

36

33 MEDITERRANEAN DANCER

She shimmies, shakes and grooves.
In her exotic outfit, she has the moves.
A Mediterranean dancer is a real treat,
Entertaining everyone she does meet.

34 NATIVE AMERICAN GIRL

With beads, fringe and detailed style,
This Native American dress has been around for a while.
It's patterned after the Plains tribe, it's true,
With headband, bag and moccasin shoe.

35 ARCTIC FISHERMAN

Ice fishing is beary fun for young and old,
who love the water and of course the cold!
It's popular with the Inuit and Eskimo,
Who have to survive in lots of snow!

36 ROYAL CANADIAN MOUNTIE

When you buy this special RCMP uniform,
You'll keep the community safe and warm.
A portion of the proceeds are donated
to The Mounted Police Foundation, it's true,
What a beary nice thing for you to do!

BEARY SPECIAL THANKS

Thank you to each member of our furry family.
To our associates who share smiles and fun with our Guests every day.
To the bears behind the scenes that make it all seem pawsitively easy.
To our Guests who entrust us in creating unfurgettable family memories and new friends.
And of course, to our furry friends who aren't just stuffed animals, but our best friends.
May your heart always be filled with the teddy bear spirit.

Hylas Publishing would like to thank Melissa Segal, Lori Zelkind, Patty Sullivan, Ginger Bandoni, and John Bickenbach at Evergreen Concepts. Many thanks to Laura Kurzu, Mindy Barsky, Staci Alfermann, and of course, C.E.B. Maxine Clark.